Cash for Trash

Mary Elizabeth Salzmann

Consulting Editor, Diane Craig, M.A./Reading Specialist

Publishing Company

Published by ABDO Publishing Company, 4940 Viking Drive, Edina, Minnesota 55435.

Printed in the United States.

Credits
Edited by: Pam Price
Curriculum Coordinator: Nancy Tuminelly
Cover and Interior Design and Production: Mighty Media
Photo Credits: AbleStock, Comstock, Photodisc, Liz Salzmann, Wewerka Photography

Library of Congress Cataloging-in-Publication Data

Salzmann, Mary Elizabeth, 1968-
    Cash for trash / Mary Elizabeth Salzmann.
       p. cm. -- (First rhymes)
    Includes index.
    ISBN 1-59679-457-7 (hardcover)
    ISBN 1-59679-458-5 (paperback)
       1. English language--Rhyme--Juvenile literature. I. Title. II. Series.
    PE1517.S3523 2005
    808.1--dc22
                                                                    2005047165

SandCastle™ books are created by a professional team of educators, reading specialists, and content developers around five essential components that include phonemic awareness, phonics, vocabulary, text comprehension, and fluency. All books are written, reviewed, and leveled for guided reading and early intervention reading, and designed for use in shared, guided, and independent reading and writing activities to support a balanced approach to literacy instruction.

Let Us Know

After reading the book, SandCastle would like you to tell us your stories about reading. What is your favorite page? Was there something hard that you needed help with? Share the ups and downs of learning to read. We want to hear from you! To get posted on the ABDO Publishing Company Web site, send us e-mail at:

sandcastle@abdopub.com

SandCastle Level: Beginning

-ash

cash

flash

hash

sash

trash

We like the  .

We look at the  .

We look at the .

I like the .

This is the .

You can buy things
with cash.

The flash is black.

The hash is good.

The sash is yellow.

This is a lot of trash.

Cash for Trash

One day Nash
was picking up trash.

While picking up trash,
Nash found a sash.

18

After Nash
put the sash
in the trash
he saw some hash.

20

The can of hash
went into the trash
with the sash.

And then Nash
put in a flash.

Mr.

Mrs. Lash saw Nash
and his can of trash
with the sash, the hash,
and the flash.

She said, "Nash,
I'll buy your trash
for a lot of cash!"

About SandCastle™

A professional team of educators, reading specialists, and content developers created the SandCastle™ series to support young readers as they develop reading skills and strategies and increase their general knowledge. The SandCastle™ series has four levels that correspond to early literacy development in young children. The levels are provided to help teachers and parents select the appropriate books for young readers.

Emerging Readers
(no flags)

Beginning Readers
(1 flag)

Transitional Readers
(2 flags)

Fluent Readers
(3 flags)

These levels are meant only as a guide. All levels are subject to change.

To see a complete list of SandCastle™ books and other nonfiction titles from ABDO Publishing Company, visit www.abdopub.com or contact us at: 4940 Viking Drive, Edina, Minnesota 55435 • 1-800-800-1312 • fax: 1-952-831-1632